THE ACTION GAP

SIMON LIEBERUM

DEDICATION

To my wife Rathi Devi (Mpsych, Clinical),
who introduced me
to my brain.

CONTENTS

About This Manual	7
Tools Needed	11
User Instructions	14
Step 1: Goal	15
Step 2: Action	24
Step 3: Perseverance	37
Maintenance	45
Warranty Information	53

01

ABOUT THIS MANUAL

We live in a world of nearly endless possibilities and have more opportunities at our fingertips than any generation before us. Every place can be travelled to, every adventure can be lived, and every industry can be disrupted. We just have to do it. Everything seems possible, and yet, we dream big and do little.

We make plans without getting started, have ideas but wait for others to realize them, and begin new things just to veer off the road and give up as soon as we encounter obstacles. But it doesn't have to be that way.

This manual aims to close the gap between having great ambitions and taking action. It's meant to serve as a catalyst to make things happen.

SMALL OR BIG, THAT'S UP TO YOU.

We all know them, the ones who seem to have it—that special gift, that x-factor that lets them live their dreams. They lead different lives than the rest of us do—travel the world, start companies, or swim the English Channel. Those few seem to have mastered a force to realize their dreams, believe in themselves and enjoy a life of their own design. How do they do that? We can chalk it up to natural talent, the right connections, or plain dumb luck. Sometimes those reasons are valid, but more often than not, people who achieve their goals are people who do a few things differently from the rest of us.

In order to get a grip on this x-factor, the first step we'll have to take in this discussion is to demystify it. "If you can see it, you can be it," as Jeff Henderson says. I choose to believe that.

The great achievers of our time come from all walks of life and whether they were rich, poor, young or old, these factors did not make a difference. It boils down to very basic ingredients, a specific mindset that creates the difference. So what is this mindset that helps those few go so effortlessly from planning to taking action? To find the answers, I asked a lot of questions and read countless books. In the end, I did not have to invent new concepts of personal development to formulate an answer. Instead, I recognized three aspects that seemed to resurface during my research continuously.

For the framework, I present in this book, I focused on these aspects and removed all the other "nice to have" information that distracted from them.

What I found across various studies and the accounts of those who seem to have successfully mastered what I call an action-mindset were three primary imperatives: First, have a clearly defined goal in mind. Second, make a choice to act on it, and third, persevere. Yes—talent, skill, leadership, vision, motivation—these all matter, but what binds all the ingredients together is knowledge of exactly where you want to go, the choice to get going, and then the perseverance to stick with it, day in, day out, year after year. If you master these three imperatives, you will pick up the rest on the way.

80% IS MIND, AND 20% ARE THE MECHANICS.
—TONY ROBBINS

IN ORDER TO MAKE MY FINDINGS WORKABLE,
I TURNED THEM INTO A FRAMEWORK:

THE SEQUENCE
GOAL-
ACTION-
PERSEVERANCE
OR SHORT G-A-P.

When executed properly, the G-A-P framework will program new routines into your brain, engaging it into the action-mindset to bridge the gap between ambition and reality. Studies have shown that it takes approximately 66 days to alter or establish routines. Knowing this, you can almost feel the connections between neurons strengthening, moment by moment and over time. Once you have successfully build the first G-A-P, you will notice that you become better at taking on other things too. The more you build, the easier it becomes.

In the next section, we will explore the tools required to get started and build your first G-A-P.

02

TOOLS NEEDED

G-A-P will program routines into your mind and brain. We will make use of the brain's inner workings to get the best results. Nothing esoteric, just hard facts.

YOU CAN USE YOUR MIND, TO CHANGE YOUR BRAIN, TO CHANGE YOUR MIND FOR THE BETTER. THIS IS SELF-DIRECTED NEUROPLASTICITY.

—RICK HANSON

1x 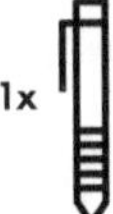   1x    1x 

1x pen,
1 x notebook,
1 x your brain

The brain consists of more than one hundred billion interconnected neurons. Each of these neurons has ten thousand connections to other neurons throughout your body. When you focus on an activity, neurons are firing, and connections are being made. Modern neuroscience teaches us that focused attention can shape our brain's firing patterns and can change the physical structure of the brain. You can use a specific focus to reinforce existing connections and establish new ones. Brain scans show that under the right circumstances, the power of brain plasticity can help adult minds grow.

Your brain:

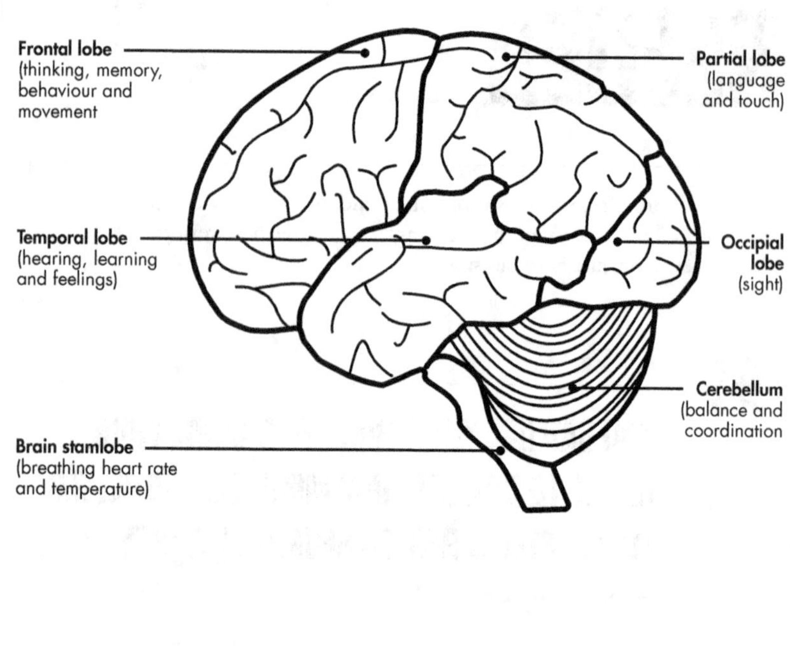

THE HUMAN BEING IS PROGRAMMED TO FUNCTION ON AN AUTOPILOT OF INGRAINED BEHAVIOURS AND HABITUAL RESPONSES AND MOVES US TO REACTIVE EMOTIONAL LOOPS AND BEHAVIOURAL LOOPS.

—DANIEL SIEGEL

Research in neuroscience indicates that most of our decisions, actions, emotions, and behaviour depend on the 95% of brain activity that is beyond our awareness.

Hence, most of our life runs on autopilot from programming in our subconscious mind. Our aim is to use these findings to choose and use the most efficient tricks, techniques, and exercises that turn our current state of mind into an action-mindset.

03

USER INSTRUCTIONS

The desired action-mindset is made of three main ingredients: goal, action, and perseverance, forming the G-A-P framework. So how do we go about building these three main ingredients?

Let's discuss these ingredients, following the sequence G-A-P. Each is a step consisting of exercises that make the framework function optimally. There is no magic involved, and there are no free rides, but I have found this to be the easiest way to achieve one's goals. Remember, your goals are yours alone, and nobody else is to achieve them for you.

START NOW.

STEP 1 - GOAL

GOAL (N.): THE OBJECT OF A PERSON'S AMBITION OR EFFORT; AN AIM OR DESIRED RESULT.

PEOPLE WITH GOALS SUCCEED BECAUSE THEY KNOW WHERE THEY ARE GOING.

—EARL NIGHTINGALE

This sounds so simple, but so very few of us get it right. Most people will agree that they know what they want, but very few put their goals on paper, in detail, and with a timeline attached. These actions make all the difference in the world.

GOAL
GOAL
1x
1x
1x
Plan goals
GOAL
Party hard
1. Choose goal
2. Make it SMART
S
M
A
R
T
3. Make reward list
4. Have goal in mind
GOAL

In this chapter, you will be guided to choose your goal and to commit to it fully. Don't be too picky; don't aim too high. Start with a smaller goal to make sure you pull through. This is about acquiring the fundamentals of the action-mindset, not about overnight success. You can replicate this technique over and over again later and set more ambitious goals.

To get meaningful results, it is absolutely crucial to choose the goals that are right for us. We are all unique individuals and should embrace our uniqueness rather than trying to imitate others' goals because we liked their results. For example, just because your neighbour is a professional race car driver and you desire his big house doesn't mean that becoming race car driver is the right goal for you to get the same result. Choose goals that are congruent with your values, your strengths, your passions, and your desired lifestyle. The results will inevitably come when the goals fall in line with your values.

For example, I value living a healthy lifestyle, so my goal is to exercise for 30 minutes daily. Value and goal are aligned. This alignment-check helps to differentiate important from unimportant goals. And even if my goal changes to, let's say, playing tennis twice a week, it is still in line with what I stand for: a healthy lifestyle. Alignment with your values is an inexhaustible source of motivation.

From a neuroscientific perspective, values play an important role too. Your brain physically modifies itself when you are participating in activities you're passionate about. When you are passionate about something, you're more likely to be captivated, driven, and ready for action and your brain releases chemical messages responsible for changes in the brain structure. Conversely, when you are disinterested, distracted, and disconnected, your brain does not release these chemicals responsible for changes in the brain structure.

SIMPLY PUT, WHEN YOU STRIVE FOR A GOAL THAT IS ESSENTIAL TO YOU, YOU WILL BE DRIVEN, FOCUSED AND MORE MOTIVATED TO ACHIEVE THAT, AND UNCONSCIOUSLY CHANGING YOUR BRAIN STRUCTURE FOR THE BETTER IN THE PROCESS.

What are some things that are inspirational or significant to you? Allow yourself to reflect and be honest.

CREATING SMART GOALS IN 6 STEPS

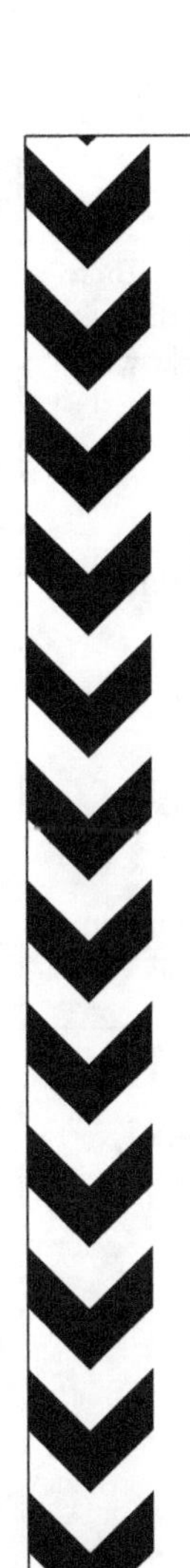

CHOOSING A GOAL THE SMART WAY

The SMART goal technique is a helpful tool to prevent you from seeking unrealistic goals or goals that are not aligned with your values and beliefs.

A SMART goal must be:

S = **SPECIFIC**
with a precise outcome

M = **MEASURABLE**
using a defined figure to
determine if the objective has been achieved

A = **ACHIEVABLE**
realistic, given the resources available

R = **RELEVANT**
directly linked to overall values and other goals

T = **TIME SPECIFIC**
a timeline of when the objective is expected
to be achieved)

Let's make this a little more clear by using an example.

Example Goal: I want to live a healthier lifestyle and exercise regularly. Therefore, I would run after work for 30 minutes, 5 times a week. I will do this with my wife. We would run from our home to the nearby park and back, which amounts to 2 km at a comfortable speed.

Why is this SMART?

Specific:	Run after work for 30 minutes, 5 times a week for 2 km.
Measurable:	Time, frequency, and distance are all measurable.
Achievable:	I have the time, the running shoes, and the required physical fitness to run 2 km.
Relevant:	Daily exercise (i.e., running) is aligned with my value of a healthy lifestyle.
Time specific:	5 times a week, starting now. No room for procrastination.

IF YOU DO NOT IMMEDIATELY KNOW WHAT TO START, IT CAN BE HELPFUL TO DO A TEST SMART GOAL WITH SOMETHING THAT COMES TO YOUR MIND EASILY.

EXERCISE 1: YOUR GOAL

On next page, you will write down the goal that you chose and fully commit to it. Glue in an image that represents this goal for you. Find a supporter to whom you will explain your goal, what it means to you, and the timeline attached to it. Your supporter should be willing to encourage you throughout the journey. He or she will follow up with you at the intervals of 25%, 50%, 75%, and 100% through the process.

GOAL SHEET

You:

I, ..., believe in my ability to achieve my goals and fully commit to:

....

....

....

....

[Insert an image that represents your goal]

Start date: ....

End Date: ....

Signature: ....

Date: ....

Supporter:

I, ..., understand the importance of reaching this goal for .... and I commit to cheering for him/her throughout this journey. I will follow up with him/her at the intervals of 25%, 50%, 75%, and 100% through the process.

Checkpoint 25% on ____ / ____ / ______
Checkpoint 50% on ____ / ____ / ______
Checkpoint 75% on ____ / ____ / ______
Checkpoint 100% on ____ / ____ / ______

Signature: ....

Date: ....

EXERCISE 2: FEEL YOUR GOAL

Come back to your goal sheet daily and take about 30 seconds to imagine what it feels like to have achieved your goal. How do you feel? What has changed about you as a person? Try to feel the situation, the more details, the better.

REWARD YOURSELF

Beyond working to become a happier and stronger person along the way, it's also good to put a little cherry on top of reaching a goal, a little something that helps you stay motivated on the way. Find something that is in line with your goal and that you really want. Once you reach your goal or certain milestones, you can congratulate yourself with a reward. It is very important to celebrate those moments of success and not to play them down. Your brain will remember the reward, making it easier for you to achieve new goals in the future.

Example Reward: Once I have completed the first 3 weeks of running, I will reward myself with the new running shoes that I've wanted for so long. They will motivate me, even more, to stick to my goal.

EXERCISE 3: REWARD YOURSELF

My reward schedule:

1) I will reward myself with ....

   when I have achieved ....

2) I will reward myself with ....

   when I have achieved ....

2) I will reward myself with ....

   when I have achieved ....

In the next section, we will put your goal into action.

STEP 2 - ACTION

ACTION (N.): THE FACT OR PROCESS OF DOING SOMETHING, TYPICALLY TO ACHIEVE AN AIM.

VISION WITHOUT ACTION IS MERELY A DREAM.
—JOEL A. BARKER

So here we are, having decided on a goal. But it's still not that easy to start. To throw ourselves into the challenge and leave the well-established, comfortable patterns behind us, we have to rely on force.

THIS INITIAL FORCE, WHICH WILL MOVE US TO DO THINGS THAT WE ARE NOT USED TO AND PUSH US OUT OF THE COMFORT OF OUR NORM IS MADE OF WILLPOWER.

Our brain, in all its beauty and complexity, is generally a lazy organ when it comes to change. Carrying out over one thousand trillion logical operations per second, the brain tries to avoid changes and pain when the reward is not in direct reach. Until the brain accepts the new patterns and forms them into habit, only sheer willpower can bridge the gap in between.

There is a constant battle between the part of the brain that takes care of basic impulses and instincts and the part that oversees your bigger goals and core values. Think chocolate bar versus apple for snack. Or buying that new watch versus saving for retirement. To fuel and support the part of the brain that helps us reach our goals, we can do a few simple things to train it. Then, these changes will, over time, make the relevant parts of the brain stronger and better connected—a global effect that helps us to reach other goals easily with increased willpower. For example, exercising regularly makes it not only easier to exercise but also easier to eat right, manage your finances, and get up on time in the morning. If you succeed at making one positive change, you will find that others follow because of overall improvement in your brain.

ACTION

1x
1x
1x
Action!
Snooze
z z z
1. Phisical health
2. Mental health
3. Support team
4. Be action hero

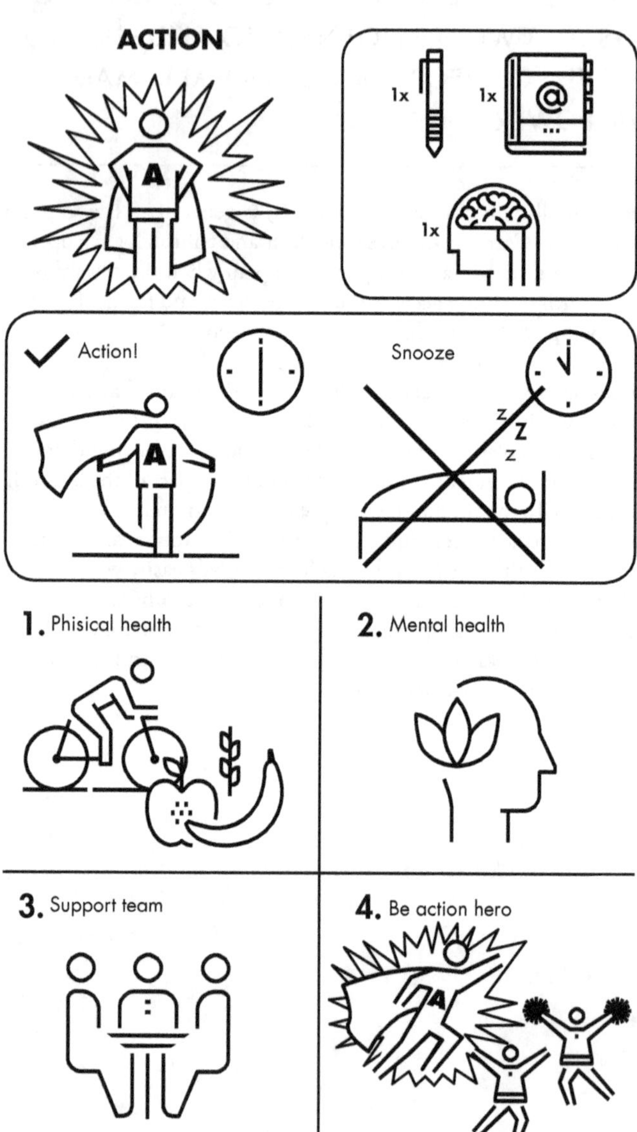

SO HOW DO WE BUILD AND MOBILIZE WILLPOWER?

Your willpower will grow as you pursue your goals, almost like a muscle that you can train. Please note that you cannot grow willpower directly; it's the work on other areas that then reflects back on your willpower. That's why it makes sense to pursue smaller goals first, grow your willpower, and increase the intensity of your goals with the increased willpower muscle. If your goal is too ambitious, you may not succeed and consequently damage your willpower muscle.

THE FIRST STEP IN BUILDING WILLPOWER IS TO UNDERSTAND THE URGENCY OF YOUR GOALS.

A good way to do that is by understanding that the future you is still you. Research indicates that we use one part of our brain when we think of ourselves and another part of the brain when we think of strangers and of our future selves. Hence, we can't relate to our future self. If we don't relate to our future self, it is easily understandable that we often ignore the consequences of our actions. Why struggle with achieving a goal today when the benefits are seized by a stranger named future you? Think of a smoker. If a smoker could fully grasp the fact that the future him/her with lung cancer is still him/her today, quitting would be easier. By making the future self feel real, we can make better decisions today.

EXERCISE 4: GET TO KNOW YOUR FUTURE SELF

Take a few minutes' time to imagine your future self. Think about the version of yourself who achieved that goal and the version who did not. Go into details on how you are going to look. How will you be dressed and hold yourself? Will you be suffering from the consequences of your choices? Do you look happy, healthy, and proud? Do you feel gratitude or regret for the choices made today?

It is crucial to do this exercise in detail. You have to understand the urgency, feel the pain of not reaching your goals. You want to look towards a future that you created actively, rather than one in which you just settled for whatever happened to you.

ONCE THE RELEVANCE OF TODAY'S CHOICES IS CLEAR, YOU CAN HELP YOUR BRAIN WITH A FEW TRICKS TO KEEP ON TRACK.

The prefrontal cortex of the brain memorises the long-term goals and core values. Less than 6 hours of sleep weaken it significantly by limiting the ability of this area of the brain to use energy efficiently. Hence, if you sleep well, your willpower increases right away. In the long-term, the prefrontal cortex gets stronger and more well-connected to the regions that it controls.

EXERCISE 5: GET ENOUGH SLEEP

A good night's sleep consists of 7-9 hours of quality sleep as well as proper sleep hygiene.

Basic rules of a good sleep include:
- Have a bedtime routine to wind down. That can include reading a book, journaling, or a hot shower.
- Be consistent with your bedtime, even on weekends.
- Avoid caffeine after 4 p.m.
- Eliminate screen time during the 2 hours before bedtime.
- Make sure your sleep environment is dark, cool, and quiet.

Similarly, meditation impacts the physiology of your brain to help you control impulses and find your motivation. Performed regularly for a couple of months, your brain will look different under a CT scan. This is especially true of the regions that help your prefrontal cortex in regulating the systems of the brain connected to giving into temptations and immediate gratification.

Research suggests that for just under half of your time, you do what is generally known as "mind wandering," meaning you are not fully focused on the task at hand. Instead, you're looking into your own thoughts.

USUALLY, WE ARE LOST IN THOUGHTS ABOUT THE PAST OR RUMINATING ABOUT AN UNCERTAIN FUTURE, BOTH OF WHICH MAKE US MISS OUT ON THE PRESENT AND FEEL UNHAPPY.

This isn't just a theory. People high on a mindfulness scale are more aware of their unconscious processes and have more cognitive control and a greater ability to shape what they do and what they say than people lower on the mindfulness scale. When you learn to make this change in your attention, you alter the functioning of your brain. This has a long-term impact on how your brain works.

EXERCISE 6: 5 SENSES

This exercise is a quick and easy method for feeling more centred on a tough day. Activating your senses reactivates the areas of your brain that help you remember your values and long term goals. Doing this daily will greatly impact your ability to stay calm and focused.

1. Sit in a comfortable upright position with your feet planted flat on the ground. Your back straight but relaxed, your hands resting on your legs.

2. Notice your breath. Take 20 seconds or so to bring the attention to each part of the breath- the inhale, exhale, and space in between. There is no need to breathe in any particular way; the body knows how to breathe.

3. Bring awareness to each of your 5 senses. Go through your senses one at a time, for about one minute each. Notice 2 things you see, hear, taste, feel, and smell. Observe them with a beginner's mind, free from ideas of what you think they should be like. Almost like a scientist, excited about every detail. The point here is to focus on the present moment and be aware of how each sense is activated at that moment.

Thoughts will come to your mind and distract you. That is normal and part of this exercise. The key is to be kind to yourself, recognise them as thoughts, and redirect your attention back to the task. Once you're finished, take a moment to notice how you feel and what has changed. Compare how you feel now with how you felt before the exercise.

People with mindfulness awareness training experience a shift in their brains towards an "approach state" that allows them to move towards rather than away challenging situations—the brain signature of perseverance. If you're really keen to shortcut the process, try the cold-shower exercise. You will see that the willpower muscle grows significantly over a few weeks' time.

EXERCISE 7: COLD SHOWER

Cold showers have an amazing effect on your willpower. Taking the first step into the cold water trains your brain in stepping out of its comfort zone, and pulling through works on your discipline. Over a relatively short period of time, you will observe that you can stick to other commitments during your day more easily. Simply put, going through discomfort makes other difficulties easier to deal with. Since you were able to beat one obstacle, the next one will be easier to overcome. It happens unconsciously. As always, start very small but consistently. Showering only the legs with cold water can be a good place to begin. Each tiny step counts.

DEALING WITH WILLPOWER CHALLENGES

The good news is that we are not exposed to temptation 24/7. Instead, there are certain times, places, and people that put us at risk to lose sight of our goals. We can study them and prepare ourselves, ideally avoiding situations that put us at risk all together.

EXERCISE 8: KNOW YOUR ENEMY

Take out your notebook and ask yourself the following questions:
1. What's the biggest obstacle to your goal?
2. When and where is it most likely to occur?
3. What can you do now to prevent the obstacle?
4. What exactly are you going to do to get back on track when the obstacle occurs?

Knowing when obstacles will occur and avoiding them in the first place gives you a huge advantage.

MAKE YOUR ENVIRONMENT WORK IN YOUR FAVOUR

You can only control your own behaviour, which is a huge challenge to willpower. External forces may work against you, especially when you are making changes. By taking control of the things that control you, you can gain back control over yourself.

CONTROLLING THE SOCIAL ENVIRONMENT

We are all subject to peer pressure. The social pressure is all around us: friends, family, colleagues, and accomplices. It might be your partner who belittles you when you want to go for that run after work or friends who don't buy into your business ideas and highlight how much more you would earn at your old job. No matter what these people's motives are, it is crucial to protect your goals from them. Your success partially depends on friends and family that will cheer you on—people who will support you and encourage you to move forward, keep focused, and keep on track. Don't accuse. Bring them on your team.

EXERCISE 9: RECRUIT YOUR SUPPORT TEAM

Identify the support system around you and decide how to get the people who matter behind you.

Example: Help your partner understand why you are working toward your goal. Explain that you are concerned about your health and that the lifestyle change really matters to you and your faith in yourself to accomplish things.

CONTROLLING THE STRUCTURAL ENVIRONMENT

Our environment is formed by our regular behaviours and vice versa. In other words, most people struggling with weight will have unhealthy food at home, and most couch potatoes will have big TVs. In order to make that change, you have to control your space. Make your good behaviour easy, and your bad behaviour hard.

EXERCISE 10: PREP THE HOUSE

Walk through your space and look out for potential dangers to your goal. Become a temptation detective and find the traps surrounding you. Get rid of them now.

Example: If you want to run after work instead of watching TV, you might want to unplug the TV or cover it with a table cloth. This small intervention might buy you just enough time to surf the urge and refocus your attention back on your goals.

Again, we need to take control of the things that control us so that we can control our behaviour. Nevertheless, you can't plan all eventualities, and sometimes, the unexpected will catch you by surprise. Distress tolerance, or in other words, the ability to stay put when things get uncomfortable, is a key factor in achieving your goals. The next exercise is the easiest and most effective method to dealing with a willpower challenge.

EXERCISE 11: RIDING THE WAVE OF TEMPTATION

Imagine temptation coming over you like a wave. It's inevitable. Don't ignore it; give it your full attention. Ride the physical discomfort. Breathe and wait it out. You don't have to act on every impulse. Have faith that if you can resist the urge for a short while, the temptation will go away like a wave that rolls past. This is your willpower gym. Do this exercise regularly, and you will become unstoppable.

Example: Stop for a few seconds before you sit on that couch instead of picking up your running shoes. Take a deep breath and feel the desire that you're about to give in. Surf it as if it was a wave. Where in the body do you feel it? Does it increase or decrease?

WHEN THINGS GO WRONG

Successful people embrace failure. They don't get it right the first time either. It's a process you'll need to learn to love. When you pursue your goals, use a scientific trial-and-error approach. That will allow you to analyse and adjust. Don't simply take my advice or repurpose someone else's perfect plan. Make it your own. Customize so that it applies to you and your goals and works best for your strengths and weaknesses within your environment. Only failure can provide you with the vital information needed to do this.

THERE IS NO SUCH THING AS FAILURE. THERE ARE ONLY RESULTS.
—TONY ROBBINS

Example: Let's say you come home from work and find yourself on the couch watching TV instead of putting on your running gear as planned. You can study the situation and identify the weak spots. Maybe you needed your running shoes to be more accessible than your comfy lounging clothes. Maybe after work is not the right time for you to exercise. Maybe you could run tomorrow before work instead. Maybe you're bored running the same route and need a change, or you need a running partner to motivate you. Use failure to make you stronger, not to be angry at yourself.

Picture your brain forming new connections as you face the challenges on your journey. Even if you fail one day, continue; don't let setbacks get in your way. Your brain helps you by taking note of the good attempts and forgetting the not-so-successful ones. For your next attempt, your brain recalls the last good attempt, makes incremental adjustments and progressively improves.

Once you have studied your failure and used the findings to prepare for future challenges (see Exercise 8), you must shake it off immediately. This may sound counterintuitive, but that's how the brain works. The harder you are on yourself when you have a willpower failure, the more likely you are to have the same failure again. Shame and guilt undermine future self-control. Feeling stressed by shame and guilt activates the areas of the brain that make us much more perceptible to immediate gratification and temptation. This is the biological opposite of what we need to remember: our long-term goals and core values.

EXERCISE 12: WILLPOWER SELF-AID KID

For this one, you'll need a piece of paper, your phone, or the blank backside of one of your business cards, something that's always with you. Write down the following 3 steps:

1. What am I feeling now? (Take 10 seconds to explore the feeling.)

2. Assure yourself that failure is normal and part of the process. (All humans are imperfect. In trying new things, there will be failures. What matters is how we deal with it.)

3. Mentor yourself. (Encourage yourself like you would encourage a dear friend when they had a setback.)

When you fail somewhere on the way towards your goal, take out the 3 steps and do them. It works.

We have limited willpower available every day. If we use it up for decision-making or impulse control, we don't have as much for whatever comes next. Plan your day ahead in detail and then execute your plan. This saves you plenty of willpower. Make sure that the toughest and most relevant parts are on top of the list so that you can face them when you still have enough willpower available.

In the next section, we will reduce our initial dependence on willpower and implement our goals into our everyday routines.

STEP 3 - PERSEVERANCE

PERSEVERANCE (N.): STEADY PERSISTENCE IN THE COURSE OF ACTION, A PURPOSE, A STATE, ETC., ESPECIALLY IN SPITE OF DIFFICULTIES, OBSTACLES, OR DISCOURAGEMENT.

> I'M CONVINCED THAT ABOUT HALF OF WHAT SEPARATES THE SUCCESSFUL ENTREPRENEURS FROM THE NON-SUCCESSFUL ONES IS PURE PERSEVERANCE. IT IS SO HARD AND YOU POUR SO MUCH OF YOUR LIFE INTO THIS THING, THERE ARE SUCH ROUGH MOMENTS IN TIME THAT MOST PEOPLE GIVE UP.
> AND I DON'T BLAME THEM; IT'S REALLY TOUGH.
> —STEVE JOBS

This chapter will equip you with the tools to keep going.

PERSEVERANCE

Steve Jobs suggests that perseverance, against all odds, is the key to success. Still, most people do not live the life they wish to and struggle to pursue their goals. And that's because it's difficult. Results come over time, not overnight, and we cannot rely on sheer willpower to carry us all the way. There exist no doubt that willpower is what gets us started, but the results come from perseverance, not from force. What's needed here is a tool that helps us turn that initial willpower into a sustainable routine, something that is so deeply anchored into our daily lives that it will take more than a willpower challenge to bring us out of it again. We aim for automation without cognitive work and the use of willpower. Imagine a life where doing sport and eating healthy happens as automatically as driving your car or brushing your teeth. That's habit!

WE ARE EXACTLY WHAT WE REPEATEDLY DO. EXCELLENCE THEN IS NOT AN ACT, BUT A HABIT.

—ARISTOTLE

We all have habits, good and bad ones. A habit is a routine behaviour that is regularly repeated and tends to occur subconsciously and automatically. Habits are wired in your brain to protect it from decision overload. Good and bad habits function the same way. Our aim is to understand these mechanics and utilize the advantage of automation for our daily life. Most successful people in the world have a set of powerful habits they practice every day.

Our brain is incredibly powerful but equally lazy. It will always choose easy over hard, which stops us from achieving our goals if the change means initial effort. The trick is to make optimal use of these inner workings in order to bypass the laziness and get our brain's power working for us. Your success in life is the sum of the habits you create, the sum of many small daily victories.

Imagine this: You develop the habit of reading only 10 minutes every night before you sleep. At a normal reading speed, that's at least 1 book per month or 12 books a year. 10 minutes isn't so hard right? Having read 12 books on one particular topic would already give you near-to-expert status on a particular topic. If you find yourself asking where to find the time for that, cut it from your TV time.

THREE COMPONENTS OF A HABIT

There is a simple neurological loop at the core of every habit, a loop that consists of three parts: A cue, a routine, and a reward.

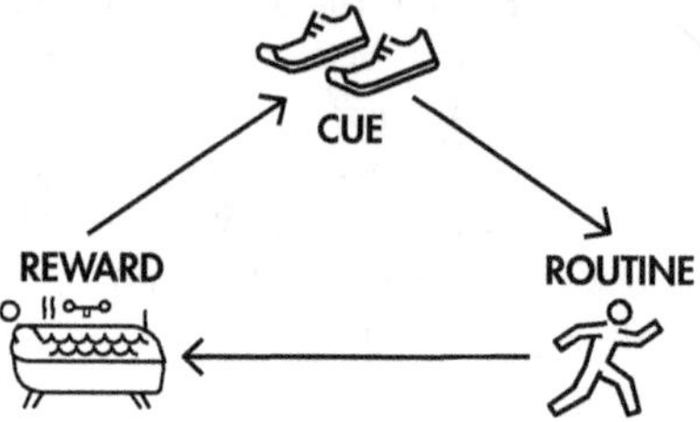

A habit is a routine our brain automatically follows: When I see a CUE, I will carry out a ROUTINE in order to get a REWARD.

PART 1 - CUE:

Habitual cues are triggers that make our brain switch to a specific program that then runs on autopilot. Cues usually fit into one of these five categories: location, time, emotional state, other people, and immediately preceding action. For example, we drive a certain route to work every morning and suddenly find ourselves heading in the same direction on a Sunday morning although we wanted to go somewhere different. Creating a cue that triggers the brain's autopilot to kick in and go for "usual" can be tricky. Therefore, we aim to connect our new habit to an existing habit. This way, we are already familiar with most of the routine; we simply need to modify it to our needs.

PART 2 - ROUTINE:

The routine is what you want to achieve, your goal or the actions that get you to your goal. For example, you want to run for 30 minutes after work, 5 times a week.

PART 3 - REWARD:

The reward must be aligned with your goal and has to be personalized to your particular needs. A reward doesn't mean that you buy yourself something every time you perform the routine; a good reward is subtler than that and must be sustainable. For the running example, the reward could be the run itself, or it could be the release of work stress or socializing with your running partner. It might also be stepping on the scale or looking at your fitter body in the mirror after exercising. Try different rewards and see what works best for you.

MODIFYING A HABIT

The brain strengthens its connections between teams of neurons representing separate moments of successive events that occur reliably in serial time. This means your brain can predict what happens next and have a continuous "associative flow." To utilize this, we want to connect the desired routine to a habit that is already established. For example, most people come home from work and change into their comfy clothes. That's a habit; it comes without having to make a conscious decision. We can rely on this to happen and therefore can anchor our new routine to it.

THE HABIT IS SO NEATLY EMBEDDED INTO OUR EXISTING NEUROLOGICAL STRUCTURE THAT DOING THE RIGHT THING WOULD BECOME THE EASIEST THING FOR OUR LAZY BRAINS TO DO.

To re-engineer a habit to our favour, we need to choose an existing habit that suits our goal and then understand its three components. Let us clarify this using an example.

EXAMPLE EXISTING HABIT: CHANGING INTO COMFY CLOTHES
I finish work every day at 5 p.m. (time), go home, and walk to my wardrobe (location) to change into my comfy home clothes (immediately preceding action). This gives me a feeling of leaving work behind (reward) before I go ahead and chat with my wife about her day (reward).

The example above is a strong chain of habits that happen automatically, without me having to remind myself to perform them. It would be hard to imagine not following this habit loop and instead, for example, spending the evening in my work clothes. Look for similar habits you can use. Once you've figured out your habit loop—the reward driving your behaviour, the cue that triggers it, and the routine itself—you can begin to modify it.

EXAMPLE MODIFIED HABIT: CHANGING INTO RUNNING CLOTHES
I finish work every day at 5 p.m. (time), go home, and walk to my wardrobe (location) to change. Instead of my comfy clothes, I put on my running gear (modified preceding action). This gives me a feeling of leaving work behind (reward) before I go ahead and ask my wife about her day as we leave the house together for our daily run (reward).

> # THE MODIFIED HABIT CHEATS OUR BRAIN TO SOME DEGREE, MAKING IT SWITCH TO THE AUTOPILOT TO CARRY OUT THE ACTIONS THAT WE FIND HARD TO DO.

Remember Exercise 10 from the Action chapter? You have to take control of the things that control you. This means that, as much as we need to avoid cues that stop us from following through, we need to install cues that support us. In the above example, it is important for the running clothes to be easily accessible. They should be positioned where I would usually find my comfy clothes so that I don't have to change my habit up to that point. I still put on the clothes that I find in a certain place. Once I'm in my running clothes and chatting with my wife about her day, things fall into place much more easily. The existing feeling of reward from the change of clothes gets transferred onto my desired routine.

EXERCISE 13: MODIFY YOUR HABIT

Identified existing habit:

Routine: ____

Reward: ____

Cue: ____

Modified habit with the desired routine:

Routine: ____

Reward: ____

Cue: ____

SLOW AND STEADY WINS THE RACE

I recommend choosing a "light" version of your habit to start with. This version is a simplified version of your new habit. The new habit has to be performed as regularly as you desire it to be in the long run. Your brain will then accept it as the new norm and switch into autopilot to perform it. The light version of your habit helps you to stick to the regular performance until your brain has accepted the new routine. Once fully established, it can serve as a fall-back option on a rainy day.

Example light version of a habit: My goal is to run for 30 minutes after work, 5 times a week. The light version would be to put on my running shoes every day after work and run on the spot for 30 seconds. That's all!
It is absolutely crucial not to over-perform here. You might say that's too easy and a waste of your time and go run instead. That's fine. But if you lack the willpower the day after, then use the light habit to stay on track. Better to start with a series of small victories and build willpower and habit rather than use pure willpower for three days of running only to relapse and beat ourselves up (which costs more willpower). It may seem a little funny just to put on the shoes and not run outside, but that's the trick. We want long-lasting change rather than short intervals that we can't sustain. Remember: If you want different results, you need to take different actions.

The light version of my modified habit is:

....

....

....

....

....

PRACTISE IN YOUR MIND

Interestingly, the required change in the brain can be achieved through mental rehearsal as well as the actual performance of the habit. Your internal representations of the routine recalled from memory are sufficient to drive plastic change in the brain.

Many top performers in sports and entertainment use mental rehearsal to their advantage. Michael Phelps, for example, was trained to watch the "videotape" to build him into the mentally strongest swimmer of all times. The "videotape" isn't real but a mental visualization of the perfect race. Phelps would imagine diving off the blocks and, in slow motion, swimming flawlessly. He would lie in bed with his eyes shut and watch the entire race down to the smallest details. Later he would not only rehearse the perfect race but also scenarios with some sort of failure and the best possible reaction to deal with them. Through these exercises, his nervous system experienced the ideal performance available for every scenario, ready to play from Phelps's mental database. In addition to the enormous training effect, this also equipped Phelps with the confidence of feeling prepared for everything possible.

EXERCISE 14: MENTAL REHEARSAL

Imagine yourself performing the desired new routine. Visualize exactly how you do it; the more details, the better the effect. It should include details like smells, mental images, sounds, and feelings that activate the senses. Imagine how it would feel if you were to do it rather than merely watching yourself as if you're watching a movie. Mental rehearsal can't make you reach your goal alone, but it can certainly help you to get there faster.

04

MAINTENANCE 

Like every other tool, your G-A-Ps need regular maintenance. I recommend the following journaling exercise to keep track and stay motivated. This way of quick journaling is used by super performers all over the world. Giving your mindset a positive spin each day can have an incredible effect in the long run.

EXERCISE 15: SPEED JOURNALING

Get yourself a small notebook. This will be your daily tracker to make sure you don't miss out on learning opportunities and to help you stay positive along the way. Dedicate 5 minutes a day, using the format below, to reflect. This will help your mind speed up the process of brain change. Put the notebook next to your bed, attach a pen to it, and do this exercise every night before you sleep. See it as an opportunity, not as a chore. It's a great way to calm down before sleeping and to end the day on a positive note. The results will surprise you.

SPEED JOURNALING TEMPLATE

____ / ____/20____   Mon   Tue   Wed   Thu   Fri   Sat   Sun

1. Return to your goal sheet and repeat your goal in front of the mirror.

2. Write down three things you are grateful for today:

1. _______________________________

2. _______________________________

3. _______________________________

3. Pick three attributes that someone must possess in order to perform your desired routine extremely well. Then fill in the statement below:

Affirmation:

I am (1)________________, (2)________________ and (3)________________!

4. Write down some positive things you accomplished:

Whom did you help today? _______________________________

What did you learn today? _______________________________

What was amazing about today? _______________________________

5. Reflect on your new habit:

Did you perform your desired habit today?

If yes, what helped? _______________________________

If no, what can you improve now so you will do it next time?

____

SPEED JOURNALING TEMPLATE

___ / ___ /20 ___   Mon   Tue   Wed   Thu   Fri   Sat   Sun

1. Return to your goal sheet and repeat your goal in front of the mirror.

2. Write down three things you are grateful for today:

1. _______________________________

2. _______________________________

3. _______________________________

3. Pick three attributes that someone must possess in order to perform your desired routine extremely well. Then fill in the statement below:

Affirmation:

I am (1)_______________, (2)_______________ and (3)_______________!

4. Write down some positive things you accomplished:

Whom did you help today? _______________________________

What did you learn today? _______________________________

What was amazing about today? _______________________________

5. Reflect on your new habit:

Did you perform your desired habit today?

If yes, what helped? _______________________________

If no, what can you improve now so you will do it next time?

____

SPEED JOURNALING TEMPLATE

____ / ____ /20____   Mon   Tue   Wed   Thu   Fri   Sat   Sun

1. Return to your goal sheet and repeat your goal in front of the mirror.

2. Write down three things you are grateful for today:

1. _______________________________

2. _______________________________

3. _______________________________

3. Pick three attributes that someone must possess in order to perform your desired routine extremely well. Then fill in the statement below:

Affirmation:

I am (1)________________, (2)________________ and (3)________________!

4. Write down some positive things you accomplished:

Whom did you help today? _______________________________

What did you learn today? _______________________________

What was amazing about today? _______________________________

5. Reflect on your new habit:

Did you perform your desired habit today?

If yes, what helped? _______________________________

If no, what can you improve now so you will do it next time?

____

SPEED JOURNALING TEMPLATE

____ /____/20____   Mon   Tue   Wed   **Thu**   Fri   Sat   Sun

1. Return to your goal sheet and repeat your goal in front of the mirror.

2. Write down three things you are grateful for today:

1. ___________________________________

2. ___________________________________

3. ___________________________________

3. Pick three attributes that someone must possess in order to perform your desired routine extremely well. Then fill in the statement below:

Affirmation:

I am (1)________________, (2)________________ and (3)________________!

4. Write down some positive things you accomplished:

Whom did you help today? ___________________________________

What did you learn today? ___________________________________

What was amazing about today? ___________________________________

5. Reflect on your new habit:

Did you perform your desired habit today?

If yes, what helped? ___________________________________

If no, what can you improve now so you will do it next time?

____

SPEED JOURNALING TEMPLATE

___ /___/20___   Mon   Tue   Wed   Thu   Fri   Sat   Sun

1. Return to your goal sheet and repeat your goal in front of the mirror.

2. Write down three things you are grateful for today:

1. ___________________________________

2. ___________________________________

3. ___________________________________

3. Pick three attributes that someone must possess in order to perform your desired routine extremely well. Then fill in the statement below:

Affirmation:

I am (1)________________, (2)________________ and (3)________________!

4. Write down some positive things you accomplished:

Whom did you help today? ___________________________________

What did you learn today? ___________________________________

What was amazing about today? ___________________________________

5. Reflect on your new habit:

Did you perform your desired habit today?

If yes, what helped? ___________________________________

If no, what can you improve now so you will do it next time?

____

SPEED JOURNALING TEMPLATE

____ / ____/20____   Mon   Tue   Wed   Thu   Fri   Sat   Sun

1. Return to your goal sheet and repeat your goal in front of the mirror.

2. Write down three things you are grateful for today:

1. _______________________________

2. _______________________________

3. _______________________________

3. Pick three attributes that someone must possess in order to perform your desired routine extremely well. Then fill in the statement below:

Affirmation:

I am (1)________________, (2)________________ and (3)________________!

4. Write down some positive things you accomplished:

Whom did you help today? _______________________________

What did you learn today? _______________________________

What was amazing about today? _______________________________

5. Reflect on your new habit:

Did you perform your desired habit today?

If yes, what helped? _______________________________

If no, what can you improve now so you will do it next time?

____

SPEED JOURNALING TEMPLATE

____/____/20____   Mon   Tue   Wed   Thu   Fri   Sat   Sun

1. Return to your goal sheet and repeat your goal in front of the mirror.

2. Write down three things you are grateful for today:

1. ______________________________________

2. ______________________________________

3. ______________________________________

3. Pick three attributes that someone must possess in order to perform your desired routine extremely well. Then fill in the statement below:

Affirmation:

I am (1)________________, (2)________________ and (3)________________!

4. Write down some positive things you accomplished:

Whom did you help today? ________________________________

What did you learn today? ________________________________

What was amazing about today? ________________________________

5. Reflect on your new habit:

Did you perform your desired habit today?

If yes, what helped? ________________________________

If no, what can you improve now so you will do it next time?

____

05

WARRANTY INFORMATION

I've learned how to fill the G-A-P. Now what?
Now, you use what you've learned!

When it hurts, most people quit, but they feel most tempted to stop when they are the closest to their goal. There will be reasons every day, very logical reasons, not to do the needful to reach your goal. From blocking beliefs to doubt and denial, your mind will throw everything it has at you. Resistance to change is hardwired in us, and it takes focus and effort to develop receptivity to change. If we don't deal with it, it deals with us and will keep us from our greater potential and purpose within. Keep your focus on your goal at all times. Don't get into reasoning with your mind. The change itself is not painful, but the resistance to it can wear down your willpower.

If going gets tough, you can use a simple but effective trick. By focusing on the pain that the journey ahead of you might bring, you bring that pain from the future into the present and thereby multiply it. Instead, fully focus your attention on the present moment—literally one foot in front of the other. By the time you have your sports shoes on and start running, it will feel much easier than you imagined it would.

AND NOW GET GOING!

ABOUT THE AUTHOR:

Simon Lieberum is an entrepreneur, traveller, avid sailor and vegan. He started his career in strategy consulting before pursuing his entrepreneurial goals in Asia. Simon married a psychologist who helped sort his head out, and he went on to combine entrepreneurship and psychology in his work. Simon now lives in Singapore with his wife and two cats.